HOW TO TEACH KIDS
ABOUT RACISM:

A Guide On How To Educate Your Child

About Diversity & Being Antiracist

REBECCA J JACKSON

TABLE OF CONTENTS

Introduction

Do you face difficulty in having a meaningful conversation with your kid about racism?

Do you feel trouble to navigate through a conversation about such a difficult topic?

Do you wonder what key messages to provide to your kid while discussing racism with them?

If the answer to any of these questions or even multiple of these questions is 'yes,' you are NOT alone. Most of the parents face difficulties in explaining their smart and curious kids the concept of race and racism. Many of them prefer not to discuss this topic proactively at home. Some of them even discourage racism-related discussions and leave their kids on their own to grapple with many doubts in their minds. But we can clearly understand that these avenues may not be the right ways to build a healthy and positive mindset.

Also, in the current chaotic environment, kids listen to words such as race, racism, prejudice, privilege, *etc.* almost everywhere. Many times, they are left wondering about the meaning of these terms. So, it has become imperative for parents to understand some simple but effective ways to establish a dialogue with their younger ones about these intricate concepts.

But starting this dialogue often seems daunting for many parents. So, I researched and compiled several simple but effective methods that can help you with this problem.

The protests born after the violent death at the hands of the Minneapolis Police of the African American George Floyd have led to vandalism attacks on various statues of historical figures throughout the world. Churchill, the English slaver Edward Colston and in recent days, several statues of Columbus and Ponce de León have been victims of a visible and media domino effect that has introduced history in a complex and legitimate debate.

The worst discussion you can have with your children about race is no discussion at all. It is certainly unpleasant to talk about race and racial injustice with young children; after all, we want to shield our children from the ugliness of the world. But unfortunately, positive discussions about race and racism should start as early as possible. Even more so now, in homes where this hasn't been a topic before, the news and the discussions you might be having amongst adults are processed by young children, they are incredibly perceptive.

Babies can notice physical differences from as early as six months. At the age of 5, children can already show signs of racial bias, favoring one racial group over another, for example. You cannot ignore or gloss over the topic, it's not a way to protect your children, but instead, it leaves them exposed to biases that exist everywhere in the world.

Children of color, unfortunately, have been probably aware for some time and have felt the direct and indirect consequences of systemic racism. Conversations about racial injustice have been part of the daily life of black families long before George Floyd.

But the recent events have brought the issues to the attention of most kids, even if they don't identify as black.

White families have to play an instrumental role in making their children aware of the inequalities and privileges from an early age.

But how do we go about it? What is the right way to talk to your children about race? After all, you are effectively telling them that the world is fundamentally unjust.

There is no easy way to do it: you will have to talk to them several times and listen to what their concerns are.

To ensure that racism does not find its way into the future of the next generation, it is up to us to take charge and educate our young ones today on the need to shun racism and embrace oneness. This is precisely what this article is meant to do.

Read on and discover some handy facts to teach your kids…

CHAPTER 1:

What is racism

What is Racism?

Racism tends to link race criteria with that of ethnicity and nationality, which is why it is often accompanied by xenophobia and nationalistic chauvinism.

There is ample historiographical documentation in which it can be shown that racism is ancient, making it one of the oldest forms of discrimination that exists.

The justifications that the racists have had have been due to motivations that focus on ethnocentric, ideological, pseudoscientific, religious, and folk criteria.

The sum of all these causes shapes the structure of racist discourse, as well as its arguments and allegations.

There is, of course, a component of prejudice and cognitive biases in which the racist ensures that he is in a superior position and that, therefore, he has the right to subdue or eliminate the inferior races.

These precepts, at the time, received a strong reception and left unfortunate consequences.

CHAPTER 2:

The importance of teaching your child young

Recognize the privileges of whiteness

Everyone should question the absence of black people in management positions, black authors in anthologies, black thinkers in the bibliography of university courses, black protagonists in audiovisual. And, also, it is necessary to think about actions that change this reality.

Realize the Racism internalized in you

As we have seen, most people admit that there is racism in America and Latin American countries like Brazil, but almost nobody claims to be racist. On the contrary, the first impulse of many people is to reject the hypothesis of having a racist behavior emphatically.

Transform your work environment

It is necessary to break with the "single black" strategy: it is not enough to have a black person to consider that particular space of power has been "detonated against racism." The slaveholding culture makes the workspace, principally racist - which also makes it one of the spaces in which the anti-racist struggle can be more transformative.

Read black authors

Even overcoming all the obstacles that accompany non-white skin and entering graduate school, the student will encounter another challenge: "epistemicide," that is, the systematic erasure of productions and knowledge produced by oppressed groups. The bibliographies of the courses rarely indicate women or black people; even rarer is that they indicate the production of black women, whose presence in the university and intellectual debate is extremely erased.

Question the culture you consume

In colonization processes, the colonizer's vision of culture was imposed, while cultural goods were looted. An example of this is the collections of the leading museums in Europe, where objects from different African, Asian and American countries are found today - pieces that, for sure, must mean a lot to these cultures.

Know your affections and desires

Black women have been ultra-sexualized since the colonial period. In the collective Brazilian imaginary, the image that they are "lustful," "easy," and "naturally sensual" spreads. This idea even serves to justify abuse: black women are the biggest victims of sexual violence in the country. The question is not about the sensuality of a certain woman, but about the need to fit black women in this stereotype.

13

Tips to Educate Children on Racism

Some tips to educate on respect and tolerance at home:

Be an example

Parents should act as they would like their children to act

Explain racism to children

Talk to your children about differences between cultures, and explain what prejudice or racism is.

Help them put themselves in the place of others

. How can we feel if we go to another country and other children do not let us play because we are from outside?

Exposing children to the difference

As we live in a multicultural and diverse society, we can participate in activities that bring us closer to other cultures. Exhibitions, festivals from different cultures (sometimes Chinese New Year, Ramadan, *etc.* are celebrated) If we already celebrate Halloween or Santa Claus, why not also visit other festivities?

Correcting discriminatory behaviors of children

If at any time our son makes a comment that seems discriminatory, it will be essential to talk to him and try to find out why he thinks so, if he has heard it somewhere, and help him see the negative of those kinds of comments. We could go back here to the point of 'how would I feel if...'

Answer and attend to their demands

It is easy to see events in the news where the accent is placed on the origin of the person who has committed a crime (a thief of X origin), so children can ask themselves questions about whether all of that origin is bad. Here it is essential to make it clear to them that no matter where you are from, that bad people are around the world, and the origin or skin color has nothing to do with it.

Power of books

Books can prove to be extremely powerful for conveying many key messages in racism-related dialogues. There are two reasons why books become a powerful tool in these scenarios

Books can have stories and kids understand things when they are conveyed through the stories

Books can have colorful visuals which makes it easy for kids to relate to the message

Books can become especially important when a kid asks you a question for which you are not adequately prepared. You can simply tell your kid that let's visit the library and explore the answer with the help of a book. And then, you can search for relevant books in your nearby library and have a significant discussion with your kid about the topic of racism.

Sometimes, you can simply buy storybooks that convey anti-racist ideas and start a dialogue with your child on your own. Similar to books, you can also use movies or videos for this purpose. You can start a dialogue with your kid when a relevant scene starts playing in the movie. Yet, my personal favorite is the use of books.

We discussed that books are useful because they contain stories. The next point talks about how you can make the stories more powerful to convey anti-racist ideas. Books can be used to convey compelling messages to kids while discussing racism. Books are influential because they contain stories and visuals.

Power of stories

Kids understand things in a better way when they are explained via stories. That is the reason books play a vital role in our topic at hand. But you can utilize one method to make the stories even more powerful. And that is – tell stories from your own experiences.

When your kids hear the stories from your experiences, they pay more attention to you as familiar characters are playing a role in the narrative.

You can only your reply with the sentence, such as - I appreciate your effort to understand these things. Let me tell you a story so that you understand it in a better way. When I was of your age, even I was confused about the same thing.

Kids will simply love to listen to the stories from your life. You can tell your experience about how you tried to understand issues around racism when you were a little kid. You can also tell stories about your friends, colleagues, or other people who are recognized by your kids.

While talking to your kids' about racism, you can utilize stories to frame your answers effectively. But even stories can become powerful when you tell them from your own experience.

CHAPTER 3:

Questions and conversations you should have with your child

How you should handle racism conversations with your kids

Parents (primarily white parents) find it difficult or uncomfortable to talk to their kids about racism, whereas for black parents living among whites, talking about racism is not an option, they just have to discuss it. But whatever reservation or fear parents may have about this sensitive issue, and the fact remains that the earlier they talk about it, the better.

Studies have shown that at a very tender age of 6 months, babies begin to notice physical differences such a skin color. And by the age of 5years, children begin to show racial tendencies such as preferential treatment of one racial group over another.

At this point, silence is not an option; ignoring the obvious leaves them exposed to racial biases in society.

Let's see how you should handle the conversation, especially after the events of the last few months, with your children at different ages. Please remember, that race isn't a one and done speech, it's a topic you will have to revisit many times and reinforce specific concepts, so make it part of a routine throughout the years that will be tackled in different ways, depending on the age and experiences of your children.

Under-five years

At this age, they may begin to notice and even point out the differences they see in people they meet. This is when you should begin to lay the foundation of the view of their world gently. Make use of words that are appropriate to their age for easy understanding.

Include the following in your conversation with them:

Recognize and celebrate differences: If your child brings up a question on skin color, use that as an opportunity to tell them that, indeed, people look different and celebrate the uniqueness of people while pointing out their similarities. Make this all fun in both your choice of words and your facial expressions.

Be open: Make them realize, in clear terms, that you're open and available to answer their questions and do not shush them when they point out persons who look different from they are. Shushing them makes it look like being different is a taboo.

Use fairness: Since they already understand the concept of fairness at this age, talking about racism as being unfair makes them realize the need to work as a team in making it better.

Do not feel bad if you do not have all the answers to their questions. It's okay.

6 - 11 years

At this age, they begin to talk about their feelings of which they need answers to. They also become increasingly exposed to information they find hard to process. At this stage, the first thing you need to do is to know what they know.

Be curious: You need first to ask questions. You may ask how their day went or what they heard in school; just show a genuine interest in knowing what is going on with and around them.

Discuss the latest happenings in the media with them: with the increasing presence of people online, it is no news then that social media and the internet may be the first places your child gets information from. Be genuinely interested in what they read and the conversation they have online. Ask to know why the media depicts certain people as villains and others as not villains.

Have an open talk: At every point in time, ensure always to have an honest and open discussion about racism, inclusivity, and diversity. This builds trust with your children and encourages them to always come to you with their questions or worries or for advice they can trust. Once this trust exists, they are more likely to discuss more topics with you.

You might argue that confronting children so early on with the problem of race is useless and possibly detrimental. But studies have shown that kids as young as 3 recognize phenotypical differences in people, and children as young as five can show racial bias.

You might have heard of Adverse Childhood Experience Awareness, also called ACEs, potentially traumatic events that are witnessed or experienced by children that have the potential to lead to adverse outcomes, both emotional and physical, throughout their life.

Most of the brain is built from birth to age three, so we know that we have to work the clay while it's still wet. That's an African proverb, or to be more specific, a Tanzanian proverb.

Because we know that, and we understand that early life experiences shape the way the brain is built, the way the brain is formed.

But how much should we share? And how should we handle the news reports of the last few months that even young children might have overheard?

We must be good mediators of media for our children at such a tender age

Remember that it isn't just new over the last few months, we can have conversations about race and racism, and we should be, ongoingly.

It doesn't require us to share the latest media story with our children, but there are conversations in a more nuanced manner, maybe in generalities, with maybe some specific messages. But it doesn't have to be focused on the specific occurrences.

Other parts of this discussion may not be appropriate for young children. We need to think about what's appropriate, and there isn0t one size fits solution: you know your children, and you know how vital this conversation and the best way to do it, and, especially, what the best entry point into that could be. Some so many parents want to talk about these issues, who want to talk about racism and discrimination and being antiracist, but they don't feel like they're experts on it. And I don't know how many people do feel like they're experts, maybe a few experts.

You need to search out and look for what could be developmentally appropriate materials, guidance that you can use with your children, to find out what you think might work.

Parents are the best judge of what is developmentally appropriate, but they can look to, for infants and toddlers, to board books. There are many of them, "A is for Activist" is a board book, for a baby to three years old; it's great because you can just read it to the child, the child doesn't have to read. Or, "Whoever You Are," a rhythmic board book about acknowledging the commonality around all of us. So, you can look by age range and by style to find the kinds of resources that are going to help you, because it is hard to try to figure it out on your own.

Also, at this age, you might start to talk about inequality and the ethnic differences, rather than racism.

Unfairness is the easiest way to conceptualize racism; you can either bring up examples from your own experience or use the "spider web activity" to make it relatable.

Give your children a ball of strings and ask them to unravel it around the room, making a very complex and tangled web. Then ask them to untangle them. They will soon discover that it is much easier to create the mess, rather than to untangle the web. You can use this visual metaphor to explain the very complicated issue of structural/institutional racism.

Use books as conversation starters. Let your children ask questions and guide the conversation. Don't just use books that depict historical facts or the struggle of black people; read books that show African Americans living their everyday lives, as well.

Expose your children to a different culture through photographs, movies, books, or cultural events and discuss the experience afterward. Make sure that your kids understand that every ethnic group includes individuals who might believe in different things and behave in different ways. Be clear that there is diversity within racial groups as well as across them.

Encourage your children to speak up about what they think is wrong. If another child makes a racist remark towards them or others, they have to be able to stand up and denounce. If you are the parents of children of color, remind them more often than ever, that they are beautiful, so that they don't internalize shame, should it happen that

23

they are called ugly; it's unfortunate, but it happens. If you are a white parent, praise the features of people of color or character of colors you might see on TV. Value physical and cultural differences; frame them as "a gift, not a liability" even when explaining that some people will view then negatively and that they might encounter racist messages.

You can also bring your children to protests, but if you feel that it might be dangerous, find other creative ways to involve children in activism. You can help your children write to a congressman/congresswoman or make signs to hang in your neighborhood.

From age 12 to 18

At this age, they can understand abstract concepts and also express their views. Their knowledge of things may be more than you can ever imagine, and they may express strong emotions on the topics they discuss.

Try to know and understand what they know and how they feel about it. Make yourself open to conversations.

Know what they know: Try to find out what they already know about racism and discrimination.

Ask questions: Whenever an opportunity to discuss racism presents itself in the news, cease it, and ask your kids what they think about it.

Introduce them to different perspectives on the subject as this will expand their knowledge and understanding of it.

Encourage action: As a lot of teenagers spend a significant number of hours on social media, some may contemplate participating in online activism. Encourage them to participate, too, as a way of responding to and curbing racial issues.

Celebrate diversity: Look for ways to introduce other cultures and people from other ethnicities to your child. Thus, it greatly helps to curb racial prejudice at an early stage in their lives and promotes cross-group friendships. Another way of introducing other cultures to them is by bringing these cultures to the home via exploring their foods, watching their movies, and reading their stories. While doing this, be very conscious of racial bias in movies and books and only select those that portray other racial groups in a positive light.

As a parent, you are your child's role model; they do what they see you and say what they hear you say. You are their introduction to the world. The best way to make them fully understand the need to fight racism is by doing so by your words and actions. So be the change or anti-racist you want to see in your child.

With tweens and teens is very important to talk about history without shying away from the truth at all anymore. It's of capital importance to introduce literary and historical figures and stories from the most diverse cultures. Simply put, your heroes don't have to look like you.

Let your children develop racial-cultural literacy; let them read and tell stories of resistance, perseverance, and resilience.

Make sure that they are aware of the harsh realities of racial inequality, but also make sure that that doesn't turn them into pessimists: every story of racial oppression is also a story of people speaking truth to power, fighting back, and sacrificing themselves for a better world. Make sure that they know change is possible and achievable. Be sure that these stories include women and children, as well; especially, if you are raising daughters, but also if you are raising boys.

At this age, children tend to be passionate, foster that passion, don't let it extinguish. You can also encourage your child to join organizations for racial justice that are of teens in your community.

If they are angry about an injustice, don't tamp it down; help him/her to make changes, even in small ways. If they decide to protest or go to a rally, let them, and accompany them if you want to.

Make sure that your children know that the struggle for racial equality is still very much ongoing and that they and your family can be a part of that struggle. The same advice as before still counts, and at this age, even more, you have to treat them as adults in conversations and be honest with your children.

Be completely honest about oppression, bigotry, discrimination, and biases, those that you might have lived, and even those that you might have inflicted and realized you did after self-reflection.

If they have diverse friends, make sure that they understand their point of view, that they can empathize with their particular situations. Make sure that the differences don't erode their friendships. White Americans have to teach their kids how to identify with the black experience and how to be good friends to black and brown youth as they grow up.

Don't shy away from political conversations at the dinner table; your children might disagree; they might rebel against your ideas; they might also teach you something. Learn to listen to them, to treat their opinions with respect, and they will do the same with others. Don't ignore hot subjects when they appear in the news; especially, violent news is a form of trauma, and it's healthy not only for your children but also for you to talk about it openly and honestly.

If they want to talk about something, don't ignore it or dismiss it, if they brought it up, it's because they need to know your opinion and share theirs. With teenagers, you can be a lot more direct and concrete about their own experiences and experiences that they are seeing and witnessing around them.

You also want to make sure that you are monitoring and addressing any inappropriate language or behavior and their social media posts. Often with teenagers, they might post or say things that they don't mean like that; but you want to catch those opportunities to help them understand that even if they didn't mean it like, it could still be hurtful to other people.

You want to foster their curiosity and intentions to make the world better, so when they ask questions about it or profess their intentions to do something about injustice, praise them. For example: "I'm proud of you that you are trying to understand what's happening, that's, so that's so mature of you to try to understand what's happening to other groups or other people."

"I'm so happy that you want to help make a change, I'm very proud that you have grown in such a principled young woman/man."

At the same time, avoid reprimanding them for questions and comments that don't quite come out the way you'd like them to: kids are curious, and they don't have the language necessarily, depending on how old they are, to phrase the question appropriately. But if you sort of smack them for asking something because they didn't say it in the way that you would have expected or you would have liked, then you will make that conversation even harder to have in the future.

So, discuss their question first, then gently correct their language. Be open and honest but try to stay calm; this is important. Many of us are very charged about this topic; it's a miserable series of events that have happened recently. But also in general and it's okay if you're angry and emotional, but label that emotion for them, so that they understand what your experience is and so that your emotion doesn't make it harder for them to participate in the conversation very importantly.

Finally, one last tip for this and every conversation that you have to have with your kids: teach, don't preach! Engage them in the discussion by asking questions, reflecting on what they've said, listening carefully to what they're saying and what they're expressing versus merely talking at them and trying to shove all of your messaging into one conversation.

How do you engage in these conversations?

We want our children to be kind, and we want our children to be compassionate and be empathic with others, but we also want our children to stand up for what they know is right. That means, having conversations and being able to, on the playground, maybe stop something that isn't right, we want to empower our children to do that for one another as well.

Just because, maybe, other families aren't having these conversations, it does not mean that what children are learning from these conversations at home should be muted. And it means that they need to talk and engage and interact with their peers in ways that advance this as well.

There are acts of racism, whether blatant or it being a microaggression, that are seen or unseen that happen to black children in their everyday experiences.

What are some of the outcomes of that, I say it truthfully, we know them all: that students don't want to go to school, that they end up not doing well, that they strike out sometimes because of how they're being treated.

They get higher levels of suspensions and expulsions, but it's not about them; it's about what's happened to them.

I'm going to make a list of the three things or specific recommendations that I believe that teachers should do:

(1) Don't expect students to be experts on any experiences beyond their own, and they're not responsible for speaking for their entire race or their entire group

(2) Make it clear that you're invested in all students succeeding and that you believe that they can, by making it clear in the way you talk to every one of them.

(3) When students have the courage, and it takes courage to let the teacher know that you have offended them by a remark or an action. Please, please, just listen to them. And don't be defensive. Try to increase your understanding through dialogue.

I genuinely believe that some teachers simply don't realize what they're doing.

But we as parents have to call on schools to teach teachers about what microaggressions are, among many things, and how to avoid them.

Parents can play a vital role in school communities to ensure that antiracism is a part of that school culture.

First and foremost, it's about advocating parents need to talk to teachers about it in parent-teacher conferences

If parents want to be intentional about antiracism, they have to be able to model.

They need to model acceptance and tolerance of differences in their own lives. They need to show that. They should be active in their schools so that they are exposing children to all different types of people that are different. It's to show their children to practice what they preach.

So be a part of the school, don't just advocate from far away, but go into the schools, read to all the children and be a part of the change.

Another complicated subject that might come up and is particularly hard to address is police brutality. After all, children often idolize police officers, and even if they don't in a certain way, to raise socially able children, and part of that is the respect for the authorities, always remembering to be mindful of your inalienable rights as an individual in a free society.

So, how do we tackle the question, "why did the police officer kill that man?"

It's dangerous for us to generalize a population in good ways and evil ways. And so being clear that there are people in the world who are good, and there are people in the world who do bad things and understanding what that means, maybe an entry point into that discussion.

There's such a fine line between wanting children to feel safe and wanting children be aware that they may not always be safe.

Remember to think about self-work, self-care, and your mental health.

We should love ourselves; we should continue to build up our families, we should continue to support each other

We know that children do better when families do better; the parents need to address their issues, often, before they can work with their children in the ways that they would want to.

To sum up, it's essential to start a process to engage in alongside children, to be able to say: "I don't know, let's figure it out together. Let's think about this together."

As far as specific language, naming what it is because when they leave your home, they're going to hear the words that are out there.

So, hearing them first from your mouth can make those conversations a lot easier: racism, privilege, bias. Talk about that and the self-reflection of what that means for you, and what that means for people close to you is a good starting point: from your own experience to share your history, whether that history is one that you'd like to change or not, is essential, especially for white parents, as children age, being able to say, I was a problem for this; here's what I've learned and here's how I've changed.

Show that capacity to change is possible and be as open and honest as you possibly can be with children.

They're going know if you're not, but also that's the respect that these conversations deserve.

And again, take it outside of just words, be able to model and be able to walk the talk that you've been having outside of your home, and outside of these conversations is so very important.

Curbing Racism and Discrimination

Just as untangling the web in the spider web activity wasn't easy, fixing racism and the menace it causes isn't going to be comfortable as well. But still, some things can be done to put it in check.

The First will be to work on ourselves. Changing our beliefs and bias that connotes racism will be a right step in the right direction. This will mean changing the way we see and talk about each other and others in society.

Speaking up in the face of racism and discrimination is another right thing for you. We must always respect and value others for who they are and be ready to support them when their values and rights are being trampled upon.

Programs should be put in place that not alleviate poverty but lift people out of poverty.

And finally, the law should be made to protect everyone and not just a selected few. All these measures are to ensure that the future of our children is guaranteed and that the issue of racism and discrimination becomes a thing of the past.

Use positive language

Sometimes, you may need to provide a historical perspective to your kids while discussing racism. In that case, you should maintain a positive tone while describing the unfortunate history of injustice and inequality. We should do this because kids have sensitive minds, and any information conveyed in a negative tone can disturb them in a significant way. I have written some key points that can help you to communicate the historical details around racism. The idea here is to provide truthful information but maintaining a positive tone

Let's assume there were two types of people of Race 1 and Race 2

People belonging to Race 2 got mistreated by some people belonging to Race 1

Because some people belonging Race 1 thought that they were superior to people belonging to Race 2

But the thought process of those some people belonging to Race 1 was incredibly wrong

So, people from Race 2 fought for their rights and eventually won the fight

Even many good people belonging to Race 1 stood for the rights of Race 2 people

Not all people belonging to Race 1 believed in treating Race 2 people unfairly

Thus, you should convey the idea that not all people belong to Race 1 mistreated Race 2 people. Those who thought that their race was superior and treated Race 2 people unjustly had a wrong mindset because all human beings are fundamentally equal. We also aim to convey the point that Race 2 people battled bravely against inequality and finally won back their right by fighting against all the odds.

If you are wondering how you can convey the equality of humans to kids, the next point illustrates that.

Always be welcoming

In today's digital age, kids are exposed to what is happenings in the surroundings to a great extent. They watch TV, surf the internet, and overheard our conversations around the dinner table. That can leave them wondering about the meaning of several terms related to racism. Kids can also be left wondering about several events.

As a result of that, kids may pose several questions to you. Many times, such questions are thrown at you when you are least prepared for them. The standard response that many of us use in such a scenario is the postponement of answering difficult questions. Some parents even make the situation worse by reprimanding their children.

But such an approach can affect the mentality of the kids in a negative way. A non-welcoming approach can discourage kids from expressing their thoughts with openness and honesty with you. So, whenever your kid wants to discuss anything about race or racism with you. Do not reprimand him. Do not discourage him. If you do not know the answer to a particular question, you can simply say - let's explore the answer together by taking the help of books or movies or a library. If you are looking for some responses that you can use to extend your support at the beginning of your answer, the responses are given in point no 3 of this book.

Kids can throw difficult questions about racism at you at an improper time or place. But even in those scenarios, you must have a welcoming approach to their questions. A non-welcoming approach can discourage kids from expressing their thoughts with openness and honesty with you.

Be Proactive

You should undertake a proactive approach regarding discussing race and racism with your kid. A proactive approach is the one where the parent utilizes every opportunity that comes to their way to make their children aware of racism-related issues. Whereas, a reactive approach is the one where a parent waits for the kid to force them to answer the questions or have a discussion.

For example, let's say that your kid has just arrived from school and they tell you that they were playing with a brown kid in the school. You may be appalled to hear racially-colored words from your kid's mouth. But mostly, your kid is just using these terms for descriptive purposes, without any malicious intent. However, this incident provides an excellent opportunity to explain it to your kid that the word that they just used is not the appropriate word to address their friend. A proactive parent will utilize this opportunity and start a conversation with the kid to reinforce a proper message.

When parents take a proactive approach, they save kids from the burden of starting the discussion. It also allows parents to frame the right message in their minds even before starting the dialogue.

However, there is a word of caution. We do not want to force our kids to have a conversation. If your kid is unwilling to talk at a particular moment, let it be. In that case, it is better not to force your kid. We should wait for another opportunity to convey the desired message.

A parent should take a proactive approach to have racism-related dialogues. This means utilizing every possible opportunity to make children aware of racism-related issues by establishing a dialogue. However, we do not aim to force our kids into the discussion. If the kids are unwilling to participate, we should wait for another opportunity.

Support

Sometimes, kids may end up framing their thoughts or questions in such a way that their sentences can come across as offensive to adults. In such situations, do not scold or rebuke your kid.

We need to understand that kids have a limited understanding of the world they live in. They also have a limited vocabulary to frame their sentences properly. So, you must extend support and encouragement to them in the beginning.

You can show your support by saying things like

I can understand your feelings

I appreciate that you are trying to understand this

I admire you that you are asking me this

Thus, you can create a wholesome and protective environment for your kid to discuss a tough topic like racism. Starting a tough conversation with appropriate support will also help you in creating a special bond with your kid. Your kid will always feel comfortable to discuss many difficult topics in their lives with you.

Your kid may end up inappropriately framing their sentences and questions while discussing racism-related topics with you. At that time, you must use encouraging replies. You should not rebuke or reprimand your kid. Your encouraging replies will create a protective environment for your kid. They will also help in nurturing your relationship with them.

Being an excellent example of anti-racist

Racism is one of the most significant problems faced in the history of humanity doing more harm than good to all. It is a curse we must all tackle before it becomes a norm. This section makes sure explanations on what it means to be an Anti-Racist and where to start teaching children to be anti-racist.

If racism means racial discrimination and segregation, the presence of a prefix (anti) connote without it, which simply means racial equality. For hundreds of years, the world has lived in a racist environment and has resulted in stiff relationships between many countries. For instance, a situation where Asians in a Black Country are given poor treatment will undoubtedly result in a poor relationship between the Asian and the Black Country. This has remained the tradition in many European and American countries where racial prejudice is the mode of the day. Over the decades, hundreds of people have lost their lives in the course of fighting against racism, while thousands have been victims in the hands of the judiciary and police. It was gathered that it is straightforward for a black or Hispanic to get picked up by the police or stopped on the road than it is for an American (due to their hatred for the other color/race).

Having noted that, what then does being anti-racist look like? An anti-racist can be best said to be that person who has fully developed, trained, and mastered his mindset to achieve whatever he wants without violating others' rights. A person who has no racism mindset sees everyone equally and not in terms of their skin and race; such people usually get ahead of life with love and support from all those around them. An instance of an Anti-Racist is Billionaire and Microsoft Owner, Bill Gates. Bill Gates is not just a Billionaire but also the most prominent philanthropist in history who has donated and given a lot to black nations and many other countries across the globe. Bill Gates has shown so much love and support for all races equally, and this is why we can see his global acceptance in the world markets. Being Anti-racist truly helps to move ahead!

Aside from Bill Gates, many other whites are anti-racist (not in the regard of President Trump) and continue to foster interracial relationships. The world has witnessed many deaths, including the recent attacks of blacks in the United States, which claimed the life of George Floyd and many more. All these can be attributed, not to failure from the side of the government, but to parents who learned racism from their parents and then passed on the same culture to their children. Racism, like every other behavior, can be learned and unlearned. It can also be taught at home by parents through the following measures:

Teaching your kids and all other kids about the dangers of racism and the benefits of anti-racism

Help children live their life daily with the principles of anti-racism

Teach children that love supersede all, and they should learn to love all races and colors equally without any form of segregation or discrimination

Make public addresses about racism and how it affects societal growth. Stand against it and promote anti-racism in society, it is easier for kids to follow your footprints if you are an excellent advocate for anti-racism than if you are not.

Talk about Racism and Anti-Racism with your kids and others

Children are the image of their parents (and the society), carrying the heritage and promoting the norms and values they have learned. This chapter clearly states how to teach children to be anti-racist by talking about both sides to them.

As young as 3 to 6 years old, children start looking at people; differently, they quickly learn the things they do and sometimes could be hard to stop them if they already mastered such acts. Racism is nothing but hatred or dislikes for a particular (or some kind of) race and skin color, not because of any evil committed by the other person. If deeply thought, the blacks who were bought into slavery committed no crime by being slaves and remaining in European and North American countries even after the abolishment of the slave trade. One can easily say it is hatred that birth racism after the slave trade.

Understanding that the mind of kids quickly learns and saves whatsoever you give to it, then parents should start taking anti-racist steps from home. To begin this exposition, use the guide below:

Just the same way families take morning devotions and prayers in their homes; parents should also find time to teach their children societal norms and wrongs. The process of teaching should include more of talking and citing examples to children. There is a high level of curiosity in children that they will always need instances and examples to prove whatever you are telling them. Note that it is in those instances they often learn and sometimes not through what you say, therefore never leave out examples.

Tell them what the world would have been like if there was no racism of any kind. Children have more tendency than adults to want to be loved; this is why they get hurt and show affection when you tell them NO. Watch entertaining and enlightenment movies that a good bond and interracial relationship with them, not the ones that portray one race as good and the other as wrong.

Let them ask questions. Children will not always understand whatever you tell them, and sometimes they might even misinterpret what you say. You still need to allow them to ask questions about what they get a wrong or what they have difficulty understanding. It is from their questions that you also get to understand the power of what you are telling (and teaching) and how well they understand you.

Always ask questions as well. According to psychologists, at some certain ages in the life of a child, they find it hard to open up to their parents or randomly walking up to them. More often than not, these are the time children need their parents most because they might need to open up to someone about things occurring between themselves and their friends or schoolmates. This is why it is advisable for you not always to talk and teach but also ask questions to your kids. Please do not wait until they walk up to you, go to them, and ask about how they are faring.

Take it slowly. If the process is too fast, you might be sounding selfish already while your children will not be getting your point. However, you should instead take it slowly and teach them in series so they can understand what dangers and harm racism have brought into the global community.

Please don't force it. At some ages (especially when a child is already exiting childhood for teenage), teaching them in sometimes hard because they are beginning to get exposed to individual acts and behaviors from their friends. These behaviors might or will be different from what their parents have taught them, but they feel it is the usual standard expected of them amongst their peers (and such behavior could extend to racist acts). If you try to force them to stop their habits, you might lose them to the hands of people who are not worth it, but because your children feel comfortable around them, they will prefer to be with such people. Also, teaching children to be anti-racist could be, at some point, tedious, but you have to go slowly and gently (with a lot of patience and tolerance) to help build the children to better people.

While your children are not the only children that should hear about racism and anti-racism, always grab every opportunity you have to talk to other kids. Perhaps your child(ren) comes home with their friends, ask them to give you a time to speak to them. Or, you can decide to joke around them while you mention what you want to talk about racism with them (do not forget always to keep it short and precise, so you do not bore them with long talks). Children's nature of curiosity is one thing that keeps them seeking for knowledge at tender ages as they want to know the truth about whatever you tell them (another reason why you should never tell a lie to teenagers especially).

Teach Your Kids to Treat People Equally (Irrespective Of Race Or Color)

Above all, to treat people equally, you must first understand how to love everyone because of who they are, not what they do or their skin color. If a racist shows hatred, then the core factor of an anti-racist is love and equality of humanity; this is why teaching your children to love all races and colors is emphasized in this context. This section examines how you can help your children and the world to have peace by teaching them to love all humans equally.

The act of treating people equally is not a virtue we were born with; by nature, everyone tends to treat people differently based on what they have done to us, the hatred we inherited from our parents, or the things we have heard about such people. A lot of behaviors and manners that kids put up are usually learned from their parents, whom they see doing such things and thereby decide to imitate their practices. The impact parents have on their kids is so evident that they can live forever with whatever they learned through them.

If we must end racism by teaching children to show love to everyone and treat everyone equally, we must show them how to do it (children learn faster through what they see). This is why you see a toddler just learning to open his mouth to speak will most likely use the same lines used by his/her parents (learning from what they see and hear). If you have two or more children in your care, now is the best time to teach these children to love others by teaching them to love themselves.

Rivalry and Hatred within The Family

Sibling rivalry is real; it is essential to teach your children to love and treat themselves fairly and help them abolish any act of bullying (either verbally or physically). If they can ideally love and understand themselves at home, dealing with the differences present outside will become very easy for them.

A well-rounded family is one with a mutual understanding; a well-rounded family is one step ahead globally. Imagine that in every family, they have ways through which they deal with each other's differences rather than yell or bully one another. They all would have mastered so much that when they come across anyone with a different idea or mindset from theirs, they will know how to handle it without causing havoc or misunderstanding. Do you want to cultivate that love and mutual understanding to help tackle racism? The lines below are the desired help.

Set an Example

You are the first person your children look up to be like (this has been well emphasized in this book). If you have a terrible relationship with your siblings, you give your kids a red light, and in some ways, they will assume since you do it with your own family, they'd want to do it too (because they want to be like daddy or mommy). If you have a terrible relationship with your siblings, it is best to make adjustments or find ways not to make it known to your children (the former is a better option, you cannot hide bad habits from your kids for too long). Also, if you put up bad behaviors like yelling at your kids or calling them bad names, you give them the chance to reciprocate that act on their siblings too (be careful how your talk to their mother or father in their presence; you are the first influence your children has).

Love Them Equally

Just like the first one, the best way to teach your children is to show it to them. Demonstrating love for your kid is one way to show them and teach them to master the act. When buying gifts, make sure you buy it equally, it is better not to buy at all than buy for the younger one and leave out on the older sibling (sometimes you can buy something cheaper for both to save cost, they know you still care about them). When you make them feel loved equally, they reciprocate the act on one another and subsequently on people they meet outside. They would say, "my daddy/mommy taught me to treat people equally."

Teach Them Patience

Just as racism is learned, patience is a virtue that can be learned too. Patience is what will hold them back from raising a hand on anyone harassing them; it takes only patience not to verbally abuse someone who is making unwarranted comments about your race or skin color. This virtue, they must first learn at home by tolerating the flaws of one another. Although patience does not come easy, and sometimes one might run out of it. However, it requires understanding, tolerance, and self-control for it to stand firm, especially when dealing with a naggy or disrespectful sibling; it is patience that holds back your harsh responses.

Encourage Playtime

Teaching them to play with one another goes a long way. It is when they play with one another that they learn some things about one another. For instance, siblings who play together will always share ideas about their friends at school or church; it is through conversations like this that they get to know who the other person is keeping friends with (either bad or good) where the parents can eventually come in to make corrections or encouragement. Families who play together always have a way to get over disastrous moments; eventually, kids learn and become useful in their world when you (the parents) are not there.

Teach Them to Share

It has been overemphasized the level of love that lies in sharing. Sharing is a kind of free will giving and philanthropic activities that children learn or unlearn from infancy (it is philanthropic because it sometimes comes out of pity and at the expense of oneself). Teaching children the spirit of sharing with others starts from teaching them to share activities, toys, wears, eating on the same plate, and many more. Once they spend time together, have something together, and get involved with each other, they begin to create memories that they will learn from when they come across other people.

Create Bonding Experiences

While it is suitable for children to be independent of one another, it is not bad if they learn to depend on one another. Give out chores to them together where they will have to share tasks and see them handle situations and conditions without your interference. When they share activities, they learn to depend on themselves, and this is a very significant sign of mutual understanding and dependence, which will make them realize why they are siblings (that they are meant for each other, that they will need each other and that they are not alone).

Teach Them Selflessness

Children usually have a way of giving absolute ownership to whatever has been called theirs, toys, space, clothes, shoes, friends, or even food. They do not always want to share these things with anybody, not even with their parents unless you insist. You can make them understand that things they call theirs are less important than people; when you teach them that they should always place human beings as more priority than material things, you not only take selfishness out of them, but you also teach them selflessness. Eventually, you will see them helping people and wanting to do favors with nothing in return; they will even give out what you have called theirs to make the other person happy.

Listen to Your Child

In the process of teaching your child to love, you must always listen to him/her. The foundation of every loving and understanding relationship is excellent listening, and this remains a great way to show your child that he deserves your time. However, make it clear to your child that the same way you give time to listen to him is the same way he should listen to people's drifts and not conclude on his perceptions. Also, to avoid your child demanding listening ears from his friends and thereby draining them of efforts and demanding unnecessarily, you must always make him stay calm (through the virtue of patience) and clearly state your points too (it must be balanced on both sides).

Learn to Give Others The Benefit Of The Doubt

Imagine driving your kid to school, and another car runs into your bumper from behind, what would you say? If you utter abusive words, your kid will observe all that you said. The next time someone grabs his snack or toy in school, do not be astonished to know that your kid unleashed terror and bullied another kid.

Why?

Because you taught your kid to get angry and abuse people verbally.

In this regard, whenever someone runs into your car or causes you expensive damage, breathe, then let your child understand that what the person did is grievous, but you are giving the person benefit of the doubt. Interestingly, there are many reasons people put up unexpected behaviors; they could be running to meet up with an appointment at work or with a medical practitioner in the clinic. This way, your kid will learn to give people the benefit of the doubt whenever they do the unexpected and will always see the best in others rather than their flaws.

Quit Gossip

The moment you start allowing your kids talk about the flaws of other kids in church, school or the boy they saw at the mall, you give them the chance to have resentments about other kids, and this can result in series of racist thoughts if they are condemning a child of a different race from theirs (they could be quick to generalize it as 'that is how Blacks/Hispanic/whites/Asians does). You might not think of that little gossip about your neighbor's black son with a poorly shaped head as racism, but eventually, your kids will have resentments about the boy; subsequently, they will likely act up when interacting with him. Know that every time you talk negatively about other people, your kids believe it is okay to do such since you do it, and they potentially hurt other people's feelings. If the situation warrants that your kid deals with relationship conflict with a schoolmate or church friend, it is best to teach him how to do that without trash-talking the other person (there are many polite ways to settle conflicts without offending the next person). This way, they also show love regardless of the person and situation, thereby keeping a small problem from ending up as a big one.

51

Treat Everyone Equally

Here is another assumption, you are out in the eatery with your kid; if the waiter seems somewhat rude, how will you react? Will you treat the waiter the same way you treat your kid's teacher, or would you give out a different treatment? Are you going to show one more respect and love than the other? Whatever you do is what your kid sees, and that is what will determine how he will react if the school cleaner yells at him. It is effortless to say you treat people equally, but in reality, is everyone equal in your sight? When you decide to make the waiter feel like he is just as same as the teacher in your kid's school, you do not only impact on your child, you also show the waiter how well you appreciate his services and understand how hard it could be serving different kinds of human.

Encourage Random Acts of Kindness

No matter your personality or the kind of person you are, people will always offer to help you. You might have some thin wallet and now imagine that someone renders a very great help to you during such times. For instance, a person mowed your overgrown lawn which you could have mowed with some money (that you do not have at the moment), someone buys you a drink, or offered to render help on your house cleaning or house chores, it will be very polite of you to appreciate such persons. Similarly, whenever your kid helps another person or does something voluntarily, you can offer to buy him a toy he admires or take him to see his favorite movie.

If you can fully implement more the things contained in this guide, you will surely help build an anti-racist legacy through your kid.

Parents who want their children not to be racist, generally don't speak with their children about race, they avoid the conversation altogether, glossing over racial inequalities and the social dynamics. These kids will be taught to be racist by society. If you avoid the subject, you are raising a kid to be racist.

If you raise a child to an antiracist, you have to deliberately encourage them to talk about race, racism, injustice, and inequality. You have to prepare then from the world intentionally they are living in and that they will inherit.

How to raise anti-racist kids

What's more, don't edit or disgrace your youngster as they attempt to make sense of what this implies. "On the off chance that they question why somebody has 'diverse skin,' don't shush them and instruct them not to be discourteous.

Try not to make dark a messy word, and it's not. Explore discussions with tolerance and sympathy to assist them with arriving at comprehension, not control. So much white quietness on issues of race comes not from the absence of mindful; however, the dread of saying an inappropriate thing. This serves nobody."

The discussions you have with your kids about bigotry ought to be legitimate. Our children need to realize that for quite a while, dark individuals have encountered unjustified stops by police, and this is a typical piece of the dark's involvement with the U.S. furthermore, in numerous different nations. They have to realize that police severity and killing of dark individuals has continued for quite a while and that the police are seldom considered answerable for it. We have to reveal to them this is a piece of the explanation dark individuals and their partners are ascending now, that they have been encountering outrage and torment for quite a while. Insufficient white individuals have paid attention to it.

In case you don't know which movies are age-or stage-suitable for your child, watch them yourself first and afterward choose.

In any case, demonstrating hostile to prejudice goes past the media you expend. Ask yourself a couple of significant inquiries:

Do your youngsters have any non-white individuals throughout their life? Do you have any companions for shading? If not, why not? Also, would you be able to change that?

Search for chances to purchase from dark organizations, both locally and on the web. Give grassroots racial equity associations, which, to a great extent, work to no end.

Follow and feature dark activists, and if your children are mature enough to have web-based life accounts, urge them to do likewise.

Start awkward discussions about bias with white loved ones. "You have to start these discussions, so the race isn't a subject just tended to after a dark individual has been abused," says racial and atmosphere equity advocate Marie Beecham. "Be proactive instead of receptive." When somebody says something supremacist in your organization, get it out. Furthermore, don't hold up until your children are out of the room. They have to realize this is the proper activity.

Regardless of how awkward this discussion is, it fails to measure up to the uneasiness dark individuals and ethnic minorities feel each time they go out. "Each non-white individual who needs to stress over running into a police officer each time they go out, who needs to feel the disgrace when a white individual goes across the street strolling past them around evening time, who needs to ponder whether the explanation they didn't land that position isn't a result of the substance of their psyche, yet the shade of their skin.

Let the irrelevance of your inconvenience stand distinctly against this, and permit this to fuel your boldness."

Simultaneously, don't hope to have the option to change each mind. Your responsibility is to keep showing up for quite a while and being an excellent example for your children.

Start with accomplishing the work on yourself, take a gander at your inclinations, start your program, and carry your kids with you. Try not to stress such a significant amount over persuading others; they have to go on their excursion.

CHAPTER 4:

Racism and police brutality and ways you can explain this to a child

Minneapolis police brutality, which led to the death of George Floyd, has instigated public outcry, a call for social justice, and a movement for people of color in the US and all over the world.

The outcry led to several protests and public opinions on the media about a change in policies in that regard. Similarly, white families have felt the pressure waves more as they are in the midst of social media conversations requiring honest opinions about racism and the fact that black children are more vulnerable because they don't know about racism but experience it later.

Spearheading these necessary conversations are early childhood experts and educators. They have written op-eds on the issue, including new lists of books on antiracism for children and shared resources with parents.

Similarly, local interest in this conversation has seen several preschool and kindergarten teachers leading the discussion with active participation in helping students think critically about race and racial issues through distance learning lesson notes.

Amy Betz, who is an early childhood specialist at the University of Minnesota's Institute of Child Development, shares a similar opinion supporting the early exposure of youngsters to issues because they could learn a thing or two. Racial bias, a seemingly hard concept, could be simplified and explained in such a way that it is understandable for kids, where they learn to recognize the argument and have an opinion to destroy the wrong pattern.

"Childhood years are significant for laying the foundation of equity and justice," she said.

Examples from the Classroom

After the death of Floyd, a kindergarten teacher at Anderson United Community School in the Minneapolis Public Schools district called Jessie Begert invited her students to a video chat, where Jacqueline Woodson's "The Other Side" — children's book about two girls, the two girls have racial differences and later became friends in a divided and segregated town.

"I think, for their age category, that is all I have for them, that I teach them-I to mean, we are all different, and that's a good thing," she added, adding that her read-aloud book library has been carefully selected for the rest of the year to help kids with perspective, understanding it and framing reality.

"I can't be colorblind and assume that these youngsters are the same. Left to them, they desire conversations about differences because they have the awareness, it happens around them, and it cannot be avoided," she said. "they don't know what it means, their moral compass is not established yet. At this point, they only notice, and that's all."

A student said she saw several police officers in the neighborhood, stores already ravaged and burned. At first, she was confused, but her curiosity soon took over, and she wanted to figure everything out, farina said.

She worked closely with the student's parents throughout the weekend, offering support to assist them so that she can deal with new information about the event. The rest of the class, she included a new read-aloud on Zoom titled "Something happened in our town." The class is a virtual discussion about the buzz-race and police brutality.

When the read-aloud session is over, she requests her students to discuss the roles of an 'upstander' and how they can be one. The "upstander" is proactive, helping out another who is mistreated.

One kid said he could confront the mean person. Another felt that confrontation is scary; they concluded that an adult is in the best position to tackle lousy behavior.

"The kids need to be aware of their power. Their words and actions pack enough power too," she added. "and they have the power to choose between using it for good and bad reasons."

Avery Cartelli, who works at Parkview Elementary as a preschool teacher, sent a free video to parents about Floyd's death. She also works with younger students in the same district. The video is a major highlight of the emotions that they had spent the whole year identifying and expressing. The unfortunate tragedy, Floyd's death, is its climax. A tragedy with all the necessary ingredients like sadness and frustration.

In the video narrative, she informs the students that a man named George Floyd endured excessive force by the police; he couldn't hold on much longer and died. "George's skin color was black; the police officer's skin color was white." She repeats messages about moral values and the importance of treating people with kindness, even with their perceived differences.

To follow-up on the lesson, she introduced a video lesson about celebrating diversity using a coloring crayon analogy.

In her explanation, she talks about her excitement before she colors the animal outline. When she unraveled the first box of crayons, disappointment was written all over her because the crayons were all in blue color.

Then she uncovered a box of crayons containing different colors with a dramatic reaction showing that diversity or difference must be celebrated.

'these crayons are symbolic; they represent our friends in this virtual environment," she said. We are all different. We have unique hair texture, and the colors of our eyes are not the same. Our skin is different. Likewise, we come in shapes and sizes. And that is just awesome."

The real underlying cause of police misconduct

With the death of unarmed "black" men at the hands of "white" police, it is understandable that racism has been suggested as the underlying cause. It may very well be. There certainly has been some evidence to suggest that. For example, a recent incident where "white" police officers ranted on camera about starting a race war and buying a new rifle to kill "black" people with. There is even some history regarding policing that dates back to keep slaves under control. However, I think not enough has been said about another potential cause of misconduct by police. That is the authoritarian mindset that gets attracted to the job of policing and reinforced on the job. In that way, I believe we have not gotten to one of the real underlying causes of police misconduct, just like we haven't gotten to the real underlying cause of racism.

Mindset is always key to dealing with anyone you might disagree with or whose behavior you might not like. It is especially important in dealing with troubled and/or troublesome people. The mindset teachers have regarding troubled and troublesome students can make a huge difference in how interactions between the two unfold, whether conflicts arise or not, whether they escalate, and how easy or hard they are to resolve. The same is right for police dealing with people who may have broken laws. Even calling them Law Enforcement Officers (LEOs) suggests a much different approach to the job than calling them Peace or Public Safety Officers.

One of Dr. Ellis' four types of irrational thinking is key to understanding why an authoritarian mindset can be a set up for more conflict between police and those who might break laws, and why conflicts so often escalate with tragic outcomes. It is Demandingness. Remember that emotion is energy to move to help us deal with threats and get what we want and need. The higher the perceived threat, the more energy to move we generate. A certain amount of energy to move can be helpful because it motivates us to respond to something that might be a threat and gives us the energy to get what we want and need. As the energy to move increases, we become more reactive and less responsible. We become less likely to consider consequences before acting, and it becomes harder to access and act on advice, information, or training or learn from our own or others' experiences. This makes sense if the threat is truly life-threatening. For example, if we were suffocating. We could die in a matter of minutes. It would be helpful, even lifesaving, to generate a lot of energy to move and to react quickly. There is an old saying, "He who hesitates is lost." That can be true if a threat is truly life-threatening. It is all about surviving at any cost. However, people often make mistakes when reacting too, and sometimes that costs them their lives. The important point, though, is that people too often manufacture threats where they do not exist or magnify ones that do out of proportion to reality. That might even be easier for police to do because they are periodically exposed to real threats to their life and limb.

This is what an authoritarian mindset sets someone up to do. An authoritarian mindset believes, "You HAVE TO (NEED TO, MUST) do what I tell you to" rather than "I want you to do what I ask." Someone with such a mindset believes, "You CAN'T (MUST NOT) do that" instead of "I don't want you to do that." That sets the stage for a much more significant perceived threat if or when others do not do what we want, prefer, or desire, which in turn will cause us to generate much more emotion than is necessary or helpful. When someone does not comply with our want, preference, or desire, we are more likely to think, "HOW DARE you?". That is the mindset of people who go into a rage. Remember that a person's behavior will tend to follow his/her emotion toward a life event. It does not matter whether you are a parent, teacher, or police officer. The process is the same, and part of being human.

Dr. Ellis used to talk about shoulding on others, ourselves, and life. For example, "You SHOULD do what I tell you," or "I SHOULDN'T have to ask you twice." SHOULD could just mean "I think it would be a good idea," but it often means the same as "You HAVE TO (NEED TO, MUST) do what I tell you" and therefore is a demand of others. SHOULDN'T often really means "You CAN'T." Dr. Ellis always used to tell people to stop SHOULDING on themselves because it causes needless and unhelpful shame and guilt. I used to tell students that SHOULDING on others, yourself, or life just makes you feel SHOULDY.

We all grow up with parents who often adopt authoritarian mindsets at times, some more than others. That becomes "rutted" in our brains from repeated exposure to their comments and actions. We often will find ourselves acting just like our own parents when we have our children because of this. Some might find that disturbing, and others do not. Some simply never see the connection. Approaching life with an authoritarian mindset is a way people try to maintain a sense of control over their lives. The more threatened people feel, the more they tend to resort to being authoritarian.

I believe the job of policing tends to attract people with authoritarian mindsets much. I also suspect that those with the most authoritarian mindsets could rise in the ranks and end up being those who decide who gets hired. That would create a bias in hiring toward those with the same authoritarian mindsets. I also would expect the job itself to validate the authoritarian mindset that already existed in those who become police officers. I suspect veteran officers then encourage new officers to go with their authoritarian impulses, and those officers comply in part because veteran officers are authoritarians with new officers.

We hear a lot about police training. We even hear that police are now being trained in de-escalation techniques. Here is the problem. That training is all behavioral and not cognitive. It is possible to put your behavior where you want your attitude to be, and practicing de-escalation could modify police attitudes away from being authoritarian. The problem is that the authoritarian mindset is so "rutted" in police officer brains from a lifetime of practice and rehearsal that behavioral training may not be enough to overcome it. In a conflict situation, it would be too easy for them to slip into old authoritarian ruts, creating a much more significant perceived threat, and an emotional followed by a behavioral overreaction. Racist thinking may contribute to the perceived threat, but an authoritarian mindset may be the real underlying problem. It would take cognitive training to address this, but even then, people could still slip into old ruts at some point in the future. Therefore, there probably needs to be some changes in how candidates for policing get selected. Departments have to develop a way to avoid the authoritarian mindset bias that is probably operating now. As they say, an ounce of prevention is worth a pound of cure.

This might be the time to express the concerns I have about when protesters make demands. I can completely understand why people would get to the mental place where they feel they have to make demands. It is understandable when you have been asking for something for a long time, and it seems like no one has ever listened. That is especially true when what you are asking for is something that others already seem to have without having to ask. However, two ways are becoming demanding can backfire.

First, it can cause the protester to generate more emotion than is helpful. That can cause him or her to overreact emotionally to what is happening, and a behavioral overreaction could easily follow. As I noted earlier, Shakespeare reportedly said, "Expectation is the root of all heartache." The higher the difference between someone's expectations and reality, the higher the perceived threat will be, and the more emotion he/she will generate in response. We all have the right to want whatever we want. However, if we start to demand what we simply desire, it exacerbates the gap between our expectations and reality if or when we do not get what we wanted. That magnifies the perceived threat and triggers more emotion than is necessary and helpful. For example, anger instead of frustration, irritation, or annoyance. I suspect this is how vandalism can begin during demonstrations – how a peaceful protest can escalate into something else. If police intervene with an authoritarian mindset, it would be easy for protesters to adopt the same attitude police might have – "How dare you?". Things can escalate quickly after that in part because anger gives anyone a false sense of power, righteousness, permission, and protection. It can make otherwise smart and civil people do some stupid things. The key to keeping peaceful protests peaceful is to keep one's THINK thermostat down at want, preference, and desire and not to let it get turned up to need, necessity, and demand.

Second, there is an old saying that for every action, there is an equal and opposite reaction. Others may very well perceive demands as a threat to them. There is a difference between being assertive and aggressive. Being aggressive can be perceived as a threat, which will only trigger more emotion than might be helpful in others. When I hear protesters talk about demands, I would much rather they simply say, "This is what we want." They have a right to want what they want, especially if it is something that others have, and they have been denied. However, by starting to demand what they simply desire, they risk creating an equal and opposite reaction in others, even others who might otherwise be supportive of what they want.

CHAPTER 5:

How racism makes other people feel

Children who experience racism may develop chronic stress, which then directly leads to changes in their hormones, which causes inflammation in their bodies, which is a marker of chronic diseases.

Also, the stress in pregnancy can affect the health of a baby even before it is born. If this stress is a racism-induced one, one can only imagine how traumatic that pregnancy will be for the mother. This may result in infant mortality or low birth weight.

This explicitly means that they do not have access to proper nutrition, healthcare, and experience an overall poor standard of living. By implication, they are at risk of developing more health challenges and receiving low quality of education.

This doesn't mean that minority children living in wealthier areas are exempted. They are at the mercy of their teachers. Their teachers are punishing them over slight errors, and their abilities may be underestimated. In essence, once the teacher does not believe in them, they find it difficult to believe in themselves.

Another place racism affects children's health is in the juvenile justice system. Studies have shown that minority youth are more lie to be incarcerated (put in prison) than their white counterparts. They get to endure the emotional, health, and psychological stress that comes with being incarcerated. Also, this period changes them and the way others see them as well.

All these stresses children go through as a result of racism may not only be permanent but continue right into their generation unborn.

Apart from racism, discrimination may also stem from other factors such as religious affiliations, sex, sexual status, immigration status, etc. all of which come with their disability.

Racism takes something away from those on the receiving end - their confidence, self-esteem, and self-worth. It brings about an inferiority complex making the victims feel inadequate. Research shows that racism has a profound effect on the health and welfare of those experiencing it.

These victims may often feel sadness, anger, anxiety, and even depression. They may also find themselves withdrawing more into themselves, away from work and study, and in extreme cases, suicidal nurse thoughts (especially in places where racism is on a high).

Racism has a way of impeding one's freedom and dignity. Victims of racism, most often than not, are made to feel like second class citizens. In a society where racial hostility is prevalent, there is lacking trust and respect among citizens, and the society's value of equality and fairness becomes questionable.

Creating schedules to settle on antiracist decisions is a day by day duty that must be done with expectations. The proceeded with endeavors of every one of us exclusively can indicate an enduring change in our general public. Since racism works at different levels, we need to settle on antiracist decisions at the different levels - individual, relational, and institutional - to annihilate racism from the structures and texture of our general public.

Effect of Racism

Today, holding racist ideas is socially condemned, frowned, and disowned. But paradoxically, racism continues to gain ground. Donald Trump himself has drawn electoral revenue from his messages on white supremacy. Overall, studies show that xenophobia has grown in recent years. Nothing trivial considering that it has a series of negative consequences for ethnic minorities, affecting their physical and mental health.

Subtle Xenophobia

Racism is not only experienced in the doctor's office. There is a "daily" racism that we cannot ignore. Street attacks or racist insults are the visible faces of the phenomenon. It is not startling news of black footballers being treated like monkeys at their entrance to the stadium.

However, the subtlest racism, the one that affects millions of people daily, does not receive as much media coverage. Less explicitly expressed prejudices and social rejection are also part of the problem. Although we often turn a deaf ear. Performing daily activities such as shopping, enrolling in an activity, or passing police control can be particularly aversive to ethnic minorities. Especially when accompanied by the looks of mistrust, negative expectations, avoidance behavior, or teasing. Furthermore, popular culture can normalize racist attitudes through language. Expressions like "There are no Moors on the coast," or "You are a gypsy," are a good example.

The Brain Suffers

Chronic exposure to racism affects the functioning of brain areas involved in the control of thoughts and emotions. This leads to a series of mental disorders that mainly include depression, low self-esteem, and high levels of stress. Although anxiety, dissatisfaction with life, post-traumatic stress, and even suicide attempts are also frequent.

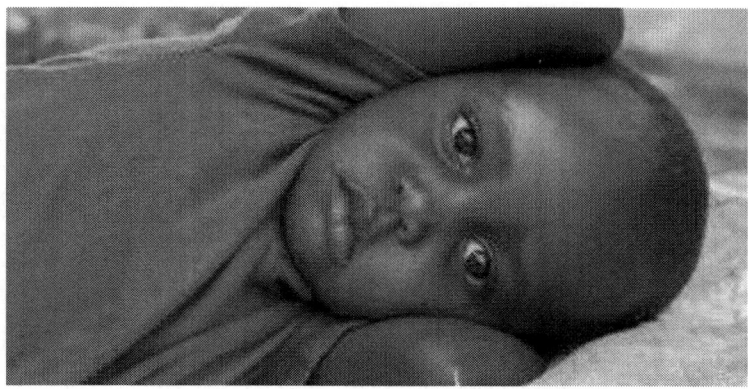

As a result, people who are victims of racism tend to be less involved in activities that improve their physical health (for example, exercising). Instead, they adopt more coping strategies that are detrimental to health (for example, consuming alcohol).

In the end, physical health suffers. The research highlights hypertension, obesity, and diabetes as the leading health problems associated with racism.

Economic Status has nothing to do

In general, people with greater purchasing power and a high educational level enjoy a better quality of life. But for ethnic minorities, having a high socioeconomic status does not guarantee better health.

In a recent meta-analysis, it was observed that age, sex, educational level, or place of birth do not affect the relationship between racism and health. Furthermore, in the United States, black people with the highest educational level have a lower life expectancy than white people with secondary education.

The Solution is in our Hands

Reducing racism and its impact on the health of ethnic minorities requires efforts at the institutional level, but also at the personal level. Motivation to reduce your biases and treat people as individuals rather than members of a particular group is key.

Research indicates that when people are motivated to make individual judgments (and not be swayed by stereotypes), they make better decisions. Their biases disappear, and they base their choices on objective facts.

Being aware of these biases and their consequences is a fundamental first step. Trying to reduce them every day is in everyone's hands.

The following are six stages you can follow:

Stop saying, "I'm not racist."

In this way, for instance, in case you're a white liberal who sees herself as "not racist," however you won't send your kid to a nearby government-funded school because the populace is dominatingly African American, that decision is racist. The antiracist position would be to, at any rate, consider enlisting your kid or potentially finding out about the inconsistencies and disparities influencing that school to battle them.

Identify racial imbalances and differences.

Racism yields racial imbalances and aberrations in each segment of private and open life. That remembers for legislative issues, human services, criminal equity, instruction, salary, work, and home possession. Being antiracist implies finding out and recognizing imbalances and aberrations that give, specifically, white individuals, or any racial gathering, material focal points over non-white individuals.

At the point when Social Security was made in 1935, for instance, it prohibited residential and horticultural laborers, most of whom were dark. While the Social Security Administration denies racial predisposition was a factor in that choice, it despite everything implied that dark laborers had less open door through the span of decades to collect investment funds and riches contrasted with white specialists. Different strategies that excessively gave "charge financed riches building openings" to white Americans created comparative outcomes for dark Americans.

So a racist examination would attribute poor or more regrettable results for dark Americans to the gathering's conduct or qualities. An antiracist examination would clarify that the issue isn't the gathering; however, the approaches that put racial gatherings at a distinct drawback.

Confront the racist thoughts you've held or kept on holding.

When you've started distinguishing racial differences, look at whether your perspectives, convictions, or casting ballot designs have legitimized racial disparity.

In case you're the parent who won't send a youngster to a transcendently dark school, consider how that decision impacts your perspectives on discipline approaches and contract schools, the arrangement gives that are profoundly interwoven with race and racism. Do you vote in favor of educational committee or city board up-and-comers who would prefer not to address instructive aberrations or neutralize nearby supporters attempting to increment instructive value? Do you realize that subsidizing arrangements influence how assets are allotted to schools and why those practices can make racial variations?

On the off chance that you don't know whether your convictions or perspectives are racist, tune in to forefront racial equity backers, activists, and associations that have laid out antiracist positions and arrangements. Let that listening brief further reflection concerning why you've had faith in specific thoughts.

Understand how your antiracism should be intersectional.

A strategy that makes disparity among white and Native American individuals, for instance, likewise yields an imbalance between white men and Native American ladies. If one accepts that dark men are better than dark ladies, at that point, that individual won't have the option to perceive how specific thoughts and strategies excessively influence dark ladies in unsafe manners.

Since race converges with various parts of individuals' personalities, including their sex, sexuality, and ethnicity, it's essential to utilize an intersectional approach while being antiracist.

Champion antiracist thoughts and strategies.

One can't endeavor to be antiracist without activity, a single direction to act is by supporting associations in your locale that are battling approaches that make racial differences. You can chip in for or finance those associations or utilize your capacity or getting into a place of capacity to change racist approaches in any setting where they exist — school, work, government, **etc.** The fact of the matter is to focus on some type of activity that can change racist approaches.

CHAPTER 6:

What is the N-word and
how to explain this to your child

Brief Historical Overview of Racism

Racism was more severe in some countries than in others. This was confirmed by Alexander von Humboldt when on his trip to Cuba, he found that blacks were better treated in the viceroyalties of the Spanish Crown than in the English, French, and Dutch colonies, and even in the United States.

However, Humboldt stressed that there was no excellent discrimination and that, after all, slavery should be abolished and eradicated.

In this way, racism served for centuries as a tool to promote a social division that was structured by castes. The dominant group was often the white race, at least as far as racial discrimination perpetrated in the Western world was concerned.

In other latitudes, similar parameters were followed in which the dominated was an inferior being or, failing that, a second-class citizen who had no access to the rights of citizens.

It was not until the 19th and 20th centuries when racism reached its final consequences. In these centuries, the extremes of genocide or apartheid systems were touched, in which blacks were free citizens, but with little or no legal guarantees.

The struggles against them resulted in their abolition and the establishment of a new order in which freedom, respect, and equality were established among men.

Factors of Racial Discrimination

Ethnocentric

Racial discrimination based on ethnocentrism is based on the premise that men who are not in the "us" ethnic group belong to the "they" ethnic group, mainly if their lineage is doubtful or mixed with other races.

For example, in Spanish America, peninsular whites called Creole whites and shore whites to those whites who, having European descent, had been born in America and who had a lower social position than those born in the Old Continent.

Ideological

It is based on ideological precepts raised with philosophy. For example, during German fascism, Alfred Rosenberg considered Hitler's thinker, who wrote a treatise in which he claimed that the "Aryan race" was superior to the Jewish.

On the opposite side of the globe, Watsuji Tetsuro argued in his book Fudo that Japan's natural environment had unique traits, which is why the Japanese were individual beings with qualities that neither Chinese nor Koreans had.

Pseudoscientific

It came to be called "scientific racism" when it was in fashion between the 19th and 20th centuries. He used pseudosciences like phrenology to misrepresent evolutionary biology concepts to build thought models that promoted eugenics and "racial cleansing."

Only whites were thought to have a right to supremacy, and supposedly "scientific" evidence was available to demonstrate this view.

None of the postulates of "scientific racism" are real, and therefore unfounded. There is no evidence to support them. Therefore, this concept is discarded and superseded without any validity in current science.

Religious

Here religious criteria are used to cement racism. Alfred Rosenberg, mentioned above, suggested that all facets of Judaism or Semitic racial aspects should be erased from Christianity, since Jesus Christ was Aryan, German, and therefore European.

Mormonism is not far behind either. In his holy book, it is stated that God stipulates that good men are white, while bad men are blacks, who are the fruit of divine punishment.

Folkloric

This cause is rare, but it exists, and there is evidence of it. It focuses on racism that practices popular culture.

This happens a lot with the ethnic group of Dogons in Mali, who, by oral tradition, fervently believe that a white, born child is a manifestation of evil spirits, and therefore must die. If he lives, he is the object of derision among his own, not knowing that such whiteness is due to a genetic condition called albinism.

CHAPTER 7:

Why are black people so angry and how to explain it to a child

There are times when we as guardians must clarify things that are difficult and uncalled for bigotry, sexism, generalizations, detest. Times when we should comfort our kids, times

I have needed to help my 10-year-old child discover that what some would do unto him isn't continuously kind or reasonable.

Talk transparently. At the point when we are straightforward with youngsters about our nation's history of bias, sexism, and generalizations, we help set them up to challenge these issues when they emerge.

A youngster who knows the racial history of the Confederate banner, for instance, is less prone to wield that image out of obliviousness.

Model value. As guardians, we are our children's first instructors. With regards to instructing resistance, activities express louder than words. At the point when you state that young men and young ladies are equivalent yet decline to purchase your child an Easy Bake Oven since it's a "young ladies' toy," what message do you send?

Accomplish something—stand firm when you witness the foul play. Challenge prejudice, fanaticism, what's more, generalizations, and urge your youngster to make a move, as well—quietness and inaction in the essences of bias overlook. Concerning hostile mascots, for instance, hold a request drive, compose an article in the school paper, sort out a blacklist of the school gracefully store, plan something for having any kind of effect.

These discussions are seldom simple, and some of the time, we don't have answers. What we do have is time, tolerance, and the craving to enable our youngsters to develop into grown-ups who esteem, what's more, respect decent variety. So, sometime in the future, they may recollect what we said the night before they began first grade — and be better individuals for it.

Kids Reaction to Diversity

We realize kids start to see racial and ethnic contrasts specifically between the ages of 3 and 5. This achieves an innocent interest that isn't yet connected to any constructive or contrary characteristics about various gatherings of individuals.

What occurs after that will be that positive and negative characteristics do come into the image passed on to kids through their folks, noteworthy others, and the broad communications.

For the most part, kids become mindful of sex early. They are beginning to take note of what they are and [what] others are and whether they ought to be dealt with unexpectedly. At first, this depends for the most part on physical appearance, as they are learning what marks you for being a kid or young lady.

They may ask, "Would she says she is a young lady? She has short hair." Or, "Would he say he is a kid? He's playing with a doll."

At that point, later, around 4, race starts to come up, when children become curious about things like skin shading. A ton of times, this is a higher amount of an issue for white larger part kids who may not be coming into contact with non-white individuals that much where they are, so for them, it's increasingly abnormal. It's exceptionally regular for them to ask guardians inquiries out in the open like, "For what reason is her skin earthy colored?" It's not exactly the equivalent for minority kids stun because they see individuals from the lion's share populace regularly. For the most part, they aren't commenting or posing inquiries about it in broad daylight so much, yet they do begin to get on special treatment dependent on race and ethnicity around this time.

Mistakes Parents/Guardian make while Educating Kids

Many guardians converse with their kids about grasping contrast; however, in unobtrusive, secret ways, they convey something altogether different. For instance, when moving toward a gathering of dark youths, a mother may unknowingly pull the youngster closer to her. Likewise, numerous white guardians frequently converse with kids about the shades of malice of partiality and separation. Yet, in their possess lives, they have scarcely any companions or neighbors of shading with whom they consistently mingle.

These verifiable correspondences are more impressive than any purposeful endeavors on the part of guardians.

Parents once in a while get excessively humiliated or self-cautious [with] children's inquiries about the distinction, mainly when those inquiries are posed openly. Guardians ought to treat them as fair requests, disclose it to them like a logical inquiry, and do whatever it takes not to consider them to be an awful thing because these inquiries are common. On the off chance that a kid poses an inquiry about somebody's earthy colored skin and the parent gets cautious or humiliated or attempts to brush the inquiry aside, that kid begins to relate that and believe, "Is there something terrible about earthy colored skin?"

Guardians of preschoolers appear to be all around educated about things like picking a protected sponsor seat of the vehicle or the significance of getting their adolescents to eat the best possible nourishments.

CHAPTER 8:

Being called racist and conversations you can have with your child about how to avoid these problems

The subject of racism is a very sensitive one, especially when dealing with children. But talking about it becomes inevitable, especially for families with "color." Failure to do this leaves your kid unprepared to deal with the issue when confronted by it in public. It is important to note that what is being discussed will depend on several factors such as the environment the family finds themselves in, their socioeconomic status, family, makeup, etc.

Whatever the case may be, each parent will have to decide what is important to them and the best approach to employ as this conversation is a must-have anyway.

The following tips below should be able to inform the parent's choice of approach:

Actually, talk about it.

This may be pretty much a routine talk for some families, whereas others may find it quite challenging to engage in it. Whatever the challenges, this conversation should not be avoided.

Failure to discuss the race at this stage of their young life makes them draw conclusions that are not only inaccurate but also equally harmful.

Some parents feel that not talking to kids about race and racism helps them see their peers as more equal to them. This is like adopting a color-blind approach to the issue, and no matter how well-intentioned this might be, it doesn't hide the fact that racism exists.

And if parents tell their kids that racism is a thing of the past, then they unknowingly let these kids feel that the racism patterns they see happen on a daily are justified.

Talking with kids about racism and the unfair treatment some people receive prepares them to be self-aware, smart, and safe out there.

Set the example

In as much as talking about racism is a great idea, setting the example is an even more excellent idea. For parents to discuss racism thoughtfully and productively, they too must be comfortable with having the conversation in the first place. They would have done their bit by actively gaining more information about the lifestyle of people different from them. Reading books on racism and watching documentaries in line with the topic better equips them for the discussion with their kids.

Apart from conversations, parents should freely connect with people of other racial backgrounds, respecting their opinions and personalities.

This will help their kids value equality the more as children mainly learn by what they see adults do. Children do not pay attention to the "do as I say" phrase; instead, the "action speaks louder than words" phrase resonates more with them. They should also encourage their children to mingle freely with other children, irrespective of their racial background and social status.

Help your child navigate their curiosity

Kids have this curious mind that could, no doubt, be annoying sometimes. The numerous questions they ask is their way of trying to understand their environment, and it's up to parents and adults to provide answers that will satisfy their curiosity - not lie to them.

It is inevitable that a child will be curious about the differences in skin color and facial appearance and will ask how this is so. That's all it is to them, curiosity, and nothing more.

They do not attach any value to their question. When they're being shushed upon asking this question, they perceive that something is wrong and would want to know what.

To give adequate answers to the numerous questions that kids ask, parents and adults need to "listen" carefully and ask for "clarifications" to get the exact meaning of their questions fully. Parents should not feel bad if they do not have the answers their kids seek, rather they should see it as an opportunity to learn together with their kids. They should also guard against who their kids ask sensitive questions, such as those bordering on racism so that they're not given answers that are disturbing or harmful to them.

Be an advocate.

Another way of leading by example is by being an advocate. This means lending your voice when it is most needed. No matter your personality and where you come from, it is essential to speak up, the little way you can, in the face of unfairness and injustice. Most times, it might not be a wrong done to us, but someone else.

By advocating, you clearly express your support towards the person(s) wronged. This leaves an imprint in their minds of what to do in the face of an obvious wrong.

At times, you may have to caution your teenage kid on the usage of certain words. They should be made to understand that there is a difference between swearing when they mistakenly hurt themselves and when they swear to bring another person down intentionally. If you do not draw their attention to these differences and reprimand them accordingly, they'll see nothing wrong in their utterances.

At other times, someone else may say something racist to your child, as a parent, you need first to warn whoever is involved not to make such statements around your kid before going ahead to talk to your child. This, too, will encourage your child to use his/her voice the more in advocating. At every point time, your words and actions should portray "anti-racist" as a parent, and a very active one at that.

The ultimate goal of speaking with kids about racism is to place humanity first before ever considering racial segregation.

Children need to realize the importance of maintaining a growth mindset in their relationship with their peers and other humans. They must be made to value the uniqueness and diversity of humanity only then can they avoid racial discrimination.

Make it relatable

It may be tough explaining racism to children irrespective of who you are. Some parents even find it damaging to talk to their kids about, especially if the kids are prone to racism attack or they have experienced racism firsthand. In this case, using concepts that resonate naturally with them becomes necessary, and that is fairness.

To kids, the concept of fairness matters a lot to them. It is, therefore, easy to use this concept to your advantage and explain to them why racism is wrong - it is not fair to some people.

However, as parents, you shouldn't just stop at raising awareness in them. Let them realize that no matter how difficult it may be, people are working hard to change the unfairness in society, and they could be a part of those goodhearted people.

Be open about addressing mistakes

Experts recommend having an open, honest conversation with kids whenever they come home offended by what they have heard or what someone said to them. They suggest it is important to let kids know that it is not in their place to educate their classmates about racism, but since they have brought up the topic, ask their opinion on it.

This open conversation aims to figure out what the child needs and weighing the options you have to fulfill the need. Just as it is important to listen to kids to understand what they say wholeheartedly, it is also necessary that we teach them how to listen to what others say and how they feel and to offer apologies once they've offended others.

This has nothing to do with being perfect; instead, it allows them to take responsibility for their actions and mistakes; thus, learning to be more aware in the future.

Validate their feelings

Whenever there is an incidence of racist violence in the neighborhood or the media, do not act like everything is alright with your kids. Check-in with them because, at that point, they're are worried and even scared that something terrible has happened to their loved ones. They are very perceptive and may not know how to express their feelings accurately.

Ask them broad questions, which allows them to express themselves. Help them engage in activities that will better help them express themselves, such as painting, writing, and drawing, amongst others.

Try as much as possible always to validate their feelings, fears, and worries and not ignore the issue at hand.

Be clear, direct and factual

Children will not be able to read between the lines, so use clear terms when speaking to them. And don't try to generalize the issue of racism by saying something like "there's unrest because some groups mistreat other groups," rather be factual and go straight to the point by saying, "there's unrest because the white people are mistreating the black people." Let them know that racial violence is terrible because they may be tempted to think that bad things only happened to black people because black people are bad people.

Help them realize that black people are also good people and that they are being mistreated. This helps them understand the actual situation at hand

Talk about history

While speaking with your kids, make them know that racism is not a new thing. Let them know that it had existed centuries back but express your hope that it'll be a thing of the past in few years to come. You may even ask their opinion on what can be done to make your hopes a reality and watch them pour their innocence to you

Explore resources

Explore the resources you have at your disposal. There are lots of materials that could help you have a better conversation with your kids on racism, explore them. Also, books can be used to introduce kids to the concept of racial diversity from a tender age and create a safe space where they can ask questions. Reading is a great way to nurture a child's mind and satisfy their curiosity.

CHAPTER 9

Why all people are equal even if they look different

Diversity is beautiful

*D*iversity is beautiful - this message tells the kids to appreciate the difference in race or color, or language. In the last point, we discussed some issues related to colorblind ideology. If parents convey this message instead of the message colorblindness, it will positively impact the mindset of kids.

You can use the following strategies to convey this message to kids effectively. You can present kids with examples of several things around them and explain it to them that the diversity of people is wholesome for society. For example, you can mention the garden, and you can explain it to kids that a garden looks beautiful when it is adorned with flowers of various colors.

You can also furnish examples of other things like toys or a box of pencils to strengthen your message.

After conveying the message that diversity of things indeed makes them beautiful, you can attempt to extrapolate the same logic and tell it to kids that It is the difference between us that makes the whole world more exciting and beautiful.

We wish to convey a message that the difference between us makes the world around us more beautiful. That way, we aim to cultivate a positive and healthy outlook in kids' minds when they see someone from different color or a different race.

The whole concept of "black" and "white" is whacked

The simple reason is that there are no genuinely white or black people. Skin color is determined by the amount of melanin someone is genetically able to produce and how much sun exposure they receive. If you look at the total population of the world, you would probably find a bell curve distribution for melanin production like you do for so many other things about humans. That means that you would have some who have a lot of something, some who have very little of the same thing, and a whole bunch of people somewhere in between. You would have some who naturally produce a lot of melanin, some who produce very little, and a whole bunch somewhere in between the two extremes.

Melanin is protective against the harmful aspects of sunlight. It would only make sense that people in our ancient past who lived near the equator would have evolved to produce more melanin than those who lived a long way from the equator. Their survival depended on it. As people moved away from the cradle of civilization, melanin production would become less critical. The further away from the equator someone got, the less they would need the protection melanin gives.

Imagine at some point in the past, fair-skinned explorers from Europe traveled to equatorial Africa. There they found groups of people with much more melanin than them and different ways of living. The contrast between the skin color of fair-skinned Europeans and equatorial Africans would have been quite striking and lent itself to generalizing that there are "black" and "white" people - even though the reality is that melanin production across the globe is more like a bell curve than an either-or proposition. The way equatorial Africans lived also made sense given where they did, but it could have been perceived as much different and even inferior in some way to the way Europeans evolved to live where they did, in much more hostile climates. Necessity is the mother of invention, and living in more hostile climates or environments would have necessitated invention, *i.e.,* brick and mortar buildings.

The bottom line is that there is no black or white race. There is only the human race with a bell curve distribution of melanin production. The ability to produce melanin is determined by where our ancestors originally came from, and how much sun exposure we get. If we lived surrounded by fair-skinned people and suddenly came across someone who genetically produced much, much more melanin than we do, it might be understandable to tend to generalize about that person, perhaps even by describing him as black as opposed to us being white. However, that is an artificial concept or abstract created by our tendency to note and attend to differences, and generalize, and even over-generalize about them. As people become more used to people around them having vast differences in their ability to produce melanin, perhaps people will finally become "color blind" and stop attending to this difference between us as human beings. It is why many see hope for the future in children who are being raised in diverse communities. Unfortunately, that has not happened yet, and sometimes it seems like it never will.

Yes, people do vary in the amount of color or melanin in their skin, and can even vary quite a bit, but that is such a small part of being human. Referring to people as Italian American, Irish, Polish, or Mexican American does the same thing. Yes, we are a great melting pot, and the ancestors of Americans came from many different places. However, distinguishing between Americans by ancestry emphasizes differences rather than similarities. Referring to some human beings as Americans and others as Germans, Russians, Chinese because of artificial human-defined geographic boundaries or language differences, is just as arbitrary as using terms like "black" and "white." When you think about history, wars have always been over differences between groups or populations of countries, and identifying people by their nation of origin was always part of the conflict.

Black Lives Matter: A Modern Civil Rights Movement

Slavery has been illegal in the United States for over 150 years. In 1964, racial segregation was also abolished in civilian areas. Nevertheless, racism is still a hot topic in America today. So current that a new civil rights movement was founded in 2013: The Black Lives Matter movement.

How It All Started: Trayvon Martin

On February 26, 2012, 17-year-old student Trayvon Martin was on his way from a supermarket to his father's girlfriend's house. He had bought a pack of candy and a can of juice when a security guard on duty in the Sanford, Florida neighborhood noticed him.

George Zimmerman, then 28 years old and himself a Latino, then reported to the police and claimed to have found a suspicious-looking man. He also suspected that he had used drugs. Since there were more burglaries in this area, he wanted to persecute the person. The police then instructed him not to do so.

At about the same time, Trayvon Martin also made a phone call. He spoke to a friend and complained to her that a menacing-looking white man was chasing him.

Shortly after that, the police received an emergency call that reported a fight. During this emergency call, a shot is heard suddenly: the security guard shot the teenager. Trayvon Martin dies at the crime scene.

Self-Defense?

The arriving police officers arrest George Zimmerman. He has a bloody nose, wounds on the back of his head, and claims to have acted in self-defense. The official responsible for his testimony, however, doubts this and writes in his report that he is demanding an arrest warrant for the security guard. However, Zimmermann is released only a few hours later because, according to the responsible public prosecutor, there is insufficient evidence against him.

Six weeks later, an official charge is finally brought against the shooter. Zimmerman has to face trial for murder. He faces at least 25 years in prison if the jury finds him guilty. However, this does not happen: On July 13, 2013, George Zimmerman is acquitted.

#BlackLivesMatter

Just two weeks after Trayvon Martin's death, numerous demonstrations took place across the country, demanding an end to police violence and racial discrimination. After Zimmerman's acquittal, the hashtag #BlackLivesMatter can also be found on social media for the first time.

What started as an online campaign developed into a national movement in August 2014. Members first gathered for a demonstration in Ferguson, Missouri, after another young black man, Michael Brown, was shot and killed by a police officer. More than 500 people took part in peaceful protests.

Since then, the Black Lives Matter movement has organized and led over 1,000 different demonstrations. In September 2016, groups from the organization were represented in approximately 40 American cities. There are also local associations beyond the borders of the USA, for example, in Canada and Ghana.

How Resistance Shaped the United States Back

With his struggle against social injustice, Martin Luther King started a mass movement that led to a change in American society. An essential part of it was organized marches, in which protests for the right to vote, equality, and better living conditions. We highlight three of the most famous protests.

The Birmingham Movement

The so-called Birmingham movement was formed in the spring of 1963 under the leadership of Martin Luther King, James Bevel, and Fred Shuttlesworth. In the protests, members spoke out against the prevailing racial segregation in Birmingham, Alabama. During the demonstrations, there were sometimes devastating acts of violence on the part of the police against the participants in the march. In particular, the abuse of children who took to the streets to integrate African American people shocked the population. It ultimately led to the demands of the civil rights movement being implemented.

This time is especially crucial for Martin Luther King because, with his success in Birmingham, the then President-in-Office John F. Kennedy and large sections of the population of the whole country began to support him.

Selma-To-Montgomery Marches

Another decisive and important moment for the civil rights movement was the three marches from the city of Selma in Alabama to the capital of the state of Montgomery. This was triggered by the so-called Jim Crow laws, under which the possibility of registering for the election was subject to certain conditions. Only citizens of a particular tax bracket were allowed to cast their votes. Illiterate people were excluded from the election, and African Americans were often threatened with violence or other consequences if they registered for the election. For example, when a group of black teachers entered the electoral register in 1963, the purely white school board dismissed them without notice.

In response, the civil rights activists around Martin Luther King and James Bevel organized a mass enrollment of 350 people, which was deliberately delayed and disrupted by those responsible. Only 25 people were admitted, and the majority of them were rejected after being checked. After these events began to pile up, the marches were organized.

The Marches

The first march took place on March 7, 1965, in response to the security forces killing a demonstrator. Some 600 people wanted to move to Montgomery from Selma but were stopped by the police outside the city and forced to quit using tear gas and clubs.

The second march started just two days later, but the capital of Alabama was not reached here either. King had called for repentance for reasons of de-escalation and fear of rioting.

The third and final march started on March 21 of the same year and lasted five days and four nights. The demonstrators traveled 86km on the highway until they finally arrived in Montgomery. The day after their arrival, 25,000 people attended a King's speech outside the State Capitol Building.

In the same year, Congress passed the Voting Rights Act, which prohibited discriminatory tests before voter registration and manipulation of new voters.

The Protest March in Chicago

The protest march in Chicago was finally directed against the big problem of missing and inhumane living space in the city of Chicago. African Americans, in particular, were prohibited from pursuing higher education and from many job perspectives or using public transport. The city was also far from paying equal and fair wages to black and white people in terms of employment and pay. However, the worst was almost the living situation in the big city, which forced many African Americans to live in inhumane conditions.

To address these injustices, Martin Luther King, James Bevel, and Al Raby led the Chicago Freedom Movement, which lasted two years from 1965 to 1967 and celebrated their glorious triumph in a new law a year later: the Fair Housing Act, the same right to affordable housing regardless of skin color or religious affiliation is guaranteed. So the Chicago movement is an excellent example of how protests can lead to legislative changes.

CHAPTER 10:

Black History and how to explain it to a child

Slavery in the United States

The slave trade in the United States was officially ended in 1865. However, the scars of this cruel part of American history can still be felt today. The transatlantic slave trade began even before the American continent was discovered.

Early Slavery

The Americans are not the inventors of the slave system. Indeed, the abduction and submission of Africans began as early as 1441. Portuguese ships captured North African Berbers and people from Central Africa and brought them to southern Portugal to do work.

A coordinated and organized trade network developed a century later when the European sea powers needed labor to manage their new colonies.

Discovery of the New World

When the American continent was finally discovered in 1491, the slavery system was by no means a new invention. However, with the settlement of the so-called New World, the scale was raised to a new level. The Indian population, the natives of North America, were enslaved by the incoming Europeans on a large scale and forced to do the most demanding physical work. The hard work combined with unsanitary living conditions led to diseases such as typhoid and measles breaking out and causing numerous victims.

Less than ten years after the discovery of America, the Spanish king permitted settlers to organize new workers. It quickly developed into a lively trade with people, which established itself as a lucrative and essential economic branch in the European colonies, the islands in South and Central America, as well as in the Caribbean.

Goods against People: The System

Over the years, a system was created to ensure a constant supply of slaves. The great European powers sailed the West African coasts with fully loaded ships. There they exchanged their goods such as weapons, textiles, horses, alcohol, tobacco, or sugar with the local tribal leaders for slaves.

105

The ships were unloaded, filled with people, and set sail for America. There the slaves were again sold at high prices or exchanged for new goods such as coffee, cotton, and spices. The ships returned to Europe, and the cycle started again.

This system lasted for almost 400 years and ensured that about ten to twelve million slaves came to America. However, this number probably only reflects the officially shipped people. The number of unreported cases is estimated at up to 40 million slaves.

Welcome to America

The passage from West Africa to America was terrible and inhumane torture for the slaves. The ships were often literally stacked up below the deck. The people were chained, lay in their excrement, and were not given enough to eat or drink. Many got sick during the lengthy crossing and, due to the high risk of infection, were often simply thrown overboard by the ship's people.

Those who survived the hardship journey were heading for an uncertain life in America. In the country's port cities, the slaves were presented to buyers. So that the hardships of the ship trip were not apparent, their hair and beard were trimmed in advance. Wounds and other blemishes were painted over so that buyers did not think their potential new slave was weak and unable to work.

Work on the Plantations

There were three major areas of work in which slaves were primarily used: agriculture, household, and mining. Working on the cotton and sugar cane plantations was often the hardest form of enslavement, but in general, the living conditions were heavily dependent on the place and the master of the slaves.

Violence was often on the list. Punishment by flogging, handcuffing, or marking with a branding iron was collective, and withholding food, and hard physical labor led to complete exhaustion of the slaves. Her so-called owner also decided whether they could enter into a relationship.

Conclusion

D iscussing racism with kids has never been an easy task. But the earlier we as parents sum up the courage to talk to them about it, the better for their emotional, physical, and psychological health.

To eradicate the trending social danger of racism, we must understand that this menace was not caused by this generation but by a faraway generation that is long gone. However, the problem persists today due to our negligence of duties and understanding that we have the power to change any unfair situations. The process of tackling racism is a collective responsibility, but it all starts with one person before anti-racism will also become a trend. Also, to curb this menace and protect the next generation, we must fully equip this generation (kids of all ages) with the required virtues and mentality to take them ahead of their racial and cultural differences. With this book being a guide, it is expected to have achieved the goal of suggesting applicable measures to raise kids to be anti-racist and subsequently curb racism.

Putting an end to racism in its entirety is an even more difficult task. The best approach remains to create awareness on the evils of racism, especially to children, and following it up with effective actions to combating these evils.

Children have always been on the receiving end of most of the injustices perpetrated by adults. Empowering them to speak up for themselves in the face of injustice is the right step in the right direction.

And the more children who can speak up for themselves, the healthier the society will become in the long run, and the more likely that the issue of racism will finally take a bow out of our lives.

Made in the USA
Coppell, TX
17 June 2021